POTPOURRI

Don't Call it Poetry

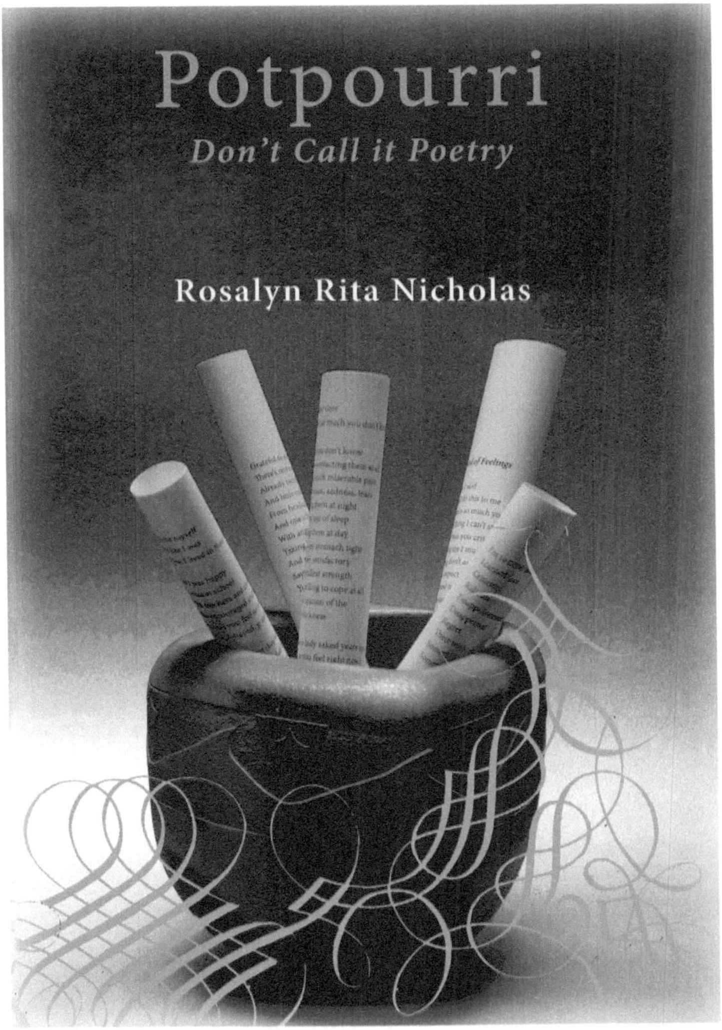

Potpourri

Don't Call it Poetry

Rosalyn Rita Nicholas

SUNSTONE PRESS

SANTA FE

Sunstone books may be purchased for educational, business, or sales promotional use.
For information please write: Special Markets Department, Sunstone Press,
P.O. Box 2321, Santa Fe, New Mexico 87504-2321.
Book and Cover Design> L.R. Ahl
Printed on acid-free paper

Library of Congress Cataloging-in-Publication Data

Names: Nicholas, Rosalyn Rita, 1950- author.
Title: Potpourri : don't call it poetry / by Rosalyn Rita Nicholas.
Description: Santa Fe, New Mexico : Sunstone Press, [2019] | Includes bibliographical references.
Identifiers: LCCN 2018059067 | ISBN 9781632932532 (acid-free paper)
Classification: LCC PS3614.I3379 A6 2019 | DDC 811/.6--dc23
LC record available at https://lccn.loc.gov/2018059067

WWW.SUNSTONEPRESS.COM
SUNSTONE PRESS / POST OFFICE BOX 2321 / SANTA FE, NM 87504-2321 /USA
(505) 988-4418 / ORDERS ONLY (800) 243-5644 / FAX (505) 988-1025

Dedication

For my beloved Family

> Husband
> Sons
> Granddaughter
>
> Relatives of the Mind

To every thing there is a season,
and a time to every purpose under the heaven:

—Ecclesiastes 3:1, The Bible, King James Version

Contents

Introduction

Throughout my life I have found that many people shy away from poetry. They say they don't like it; they don't understand it; they are afraid of it. Poetry is as popular as a rattlesnake.

I studied poetry in high school and college and have written poetry for fifty years. Naturally, one's mind and heart grow and change over time. All of us evolve. I certainly have, and still do. In reading my oldest poems, I see a young girl's innocence in some, yet a remarkable maturity and wisdom in others. I have not differentiated my poems according to age when written. Surely the reader may be able to do that, but maybe not.

After studying and living, I conclude that poetry is what one wants it to be. More than one academic has told me that what I write is not in vogue according to proper poetry experts. I am both amused and heartened by this assessment since often poets are not acknowledged in their lifetime.

I do not pretend to write in any accepted or expected style. Rather, I write for myself, for me. Poetry is my method of sharing thoughts, experiences, dreams, images, senses, feelings, memories. Some recollections are my own, and some belong to those who shared theirs with me. Some poems are mental exercises woven onto paper, while others are dreams caught before I truly woke. My writing may not be poetry, but it is honest, and it is authentic.

Poetry is what you want it to be. If you feel it, it is real. Just read aloud from line to line just as you would a book. It's not fancy, it's Potpourri.

ON FAITH

Biloxi Beach

As I walked along the pier by the beach
Up and back, up and back
So many times that crisp and windy afternoon
Gulls hid in rocky spaces, then rose
And flew near enough for me to touch
At a time in my life when
Reaching out was what I was meant to do

I rested for a while with the warmth of a Voice in my ear
Calling me to build a reservoir of serenity in my soul
Imploring me to see the answer from the pier
Where the sunlight glistened across the Gulf
With a message simple and shining

Beauty is in nature, God within ourselves
Sometimes we capture a glimpse of immortality
Just by accepting the grace of being alive

Through the Voice I was finding what I longed for
Searching for something found deep within myself
I was finding me- whole and alive and well
Full of all the love I am capable of
Full of all the joy a heart can bring
Full of all the strength I was born with
Full enough now to begin to give and give and give again

Between Sea Level and Santa Fe

Since parting of the waters was once upon a time
I wondered if miracles ever happened anymore
Searching in church but never finding them there
Looking in life between sea level and Santa Fe

He asked me to join him upon the gravel road
As the mountain patiently beckoned us onward
Among aspen leaves catching the light of the sun
Singing their song through the chill of the air

With all strength and breath taken near away
I sank embarrassed to the ground on my knees
Pondering if this was altitude or enlightenment
He leaned over when urging me—we're almost there

So I followed him up golden mountainous path
To rest at smooth rocks in the stream up ahead
Watching the infinitely beautiful world down below
Enthralled by faint fragrance of fall everywhere

I knelt o'er the brook and laid down my hand
Cupping the water so very cold to the touch
And blotted my brow and throat with the wet
Baptism and birth in simple hallowed place

He'd brought me there to view life with his vision
To belong within sacredness of his special land
Which one's the modern miracle more rare?
Gentle gift of the day—or His choice of its giver?

White Sands

At first I thought the place wasn't very much
Just millions of granules and grains of White Sands
When walking barefoot up the coolness of the hill
To the top of the dune and across one after another and another
Leaving behind the smell of greenery and the sounds of daily living
Gradually walking away from any navigational sense of the present
Walking ever toward extreme shadows of lightness and dark
To a spot deeper inside where Nothingness reigned free
No sound, no smell, no breeze, no hues, no hint of the world
Simplicity of sky and sand, blinding with brilliant purity
Nature's monument consisting of complete and absolute silence
I was standing there loving the moment more than I expected to
Feeling fulfilled and connected rather than alone or small
Receiving the gift of Life just by virtue of standing there
Watching footprints in the sands acknowledging identity
Believing they would soon enough be swept away by Time
Just as I wondered if we really mattered in the scheme of things
I was told that floods had come to this desert where we were
To cause seeds to grow where generally they would not

And for our goodbye
God granted us a glorious double rainbow

Relativity of Light

Beams of sunlight filtering through
Warmed the room and me
As darkness fell the lamps became
The way that I could see
Both sunbeams and electricity
Gave me light and view
Helping sight along, or so I thought
For all the things I knew
Came stormy rains and lightning
Cancelling all power
So slowly night enveloped me
While I bathed by shadow's hour
Dreaming of dreams, and thinking
Feeling more naked not to see
Within the pantry a candle called
And spoke as if a friend
Its flicker told of camaraderie
And love never to end
Even guardianship of me
The candle flame was so much less
Than lamp or sunbeam ray
Yet candlelight lit up my heart
For reminding me the way
When life's its very loneliest
A quiet flame is there
To warm and to comfort

Wrap me with gentle care
So small the light the candle's is
Yet large the Light to me
Though nye invisible by the day
By night is when it shows
It's always darkest 'fore the dawn
That's when my candle glows

God, Give Me the Strength Not to Hate

God, give me the strength not to hate
        and the emotions to love
Give me the self-confidence to survive
        and the humility to see my weaknesses
Give me the virtue of patience
        and the courage to dissent
Give me the sorrow to weep so that
        I may enjoy happiness all the more
Give me the Daylight to see
        the insignificance of my being
Give me the faith to always believe in You
        and the wisdom not to believe in everything

Tribute

I stand before Thee naked, full of frustration
Thou hast molded me strong of spirit and of mind
My thoughts spin madly in my head
Salty tears pour down my trembling cheek

I worship the golden bars of music
That float upon the clouds
I want to sing hymns of praise for Thee
But, alas, my voice cannot reach the notes

I feel shivers along my spine
When symphony attacks the room
I want to compose gloriously for Thee
But, alas, I cannot hear a tune

I honor the freedom, beauty, and wisdom of Man
I want to carve eternal Humanity
And offer him up to Thee
But, alas, my poor hand is unskilled

I see noble simplicity and loveliness and grace in dancing
I want to dance my feet numb for Thee
But, alas, I lack agility

God of this world, I am Thy humble servant
Wishing to adorn Thee with magnificence

But alas, I am unable

I beg to give, but with all my strength
I can never create fine talents out of air
I can speak words of love
But, alas, everyone owns the words he says

And so, I fail, despite my desperate will
To present to Thee a gift unique
A great gift, worthy of Thee

I regret my gift's so very small
But, alas, my self is all I have

Majestic Mountain

I went far, far away to a land
Of pesto and paella
Aspens and altitudes
Hopi bracelets and
Turquoise widow spiders
Nambe and button covers
Pueblos, pottery, and pinon
Sculpture smooth to the touch
Canvases brushed with color
A land smelling of saffron and salmon
Tasting of tuna and turkey
And raspberries reminding me of communion
(Awakening the soul of the schoolgirl who'd
stolen them a lifetime ago
from vines in Erlangen and Nurnberg)
It was a land of wide gorges and waterfalls
Rivers running cold
Cliffs so steep rocks came tumbling down
And mountains so mystical
Only the Medicine Man would know
Sometimes now late at night I swear I hear
His chanting through the constant
Whisper of the wind
Calling me back to the aspens
On the majestic mountain of Santa Fe

ON LIBERTY

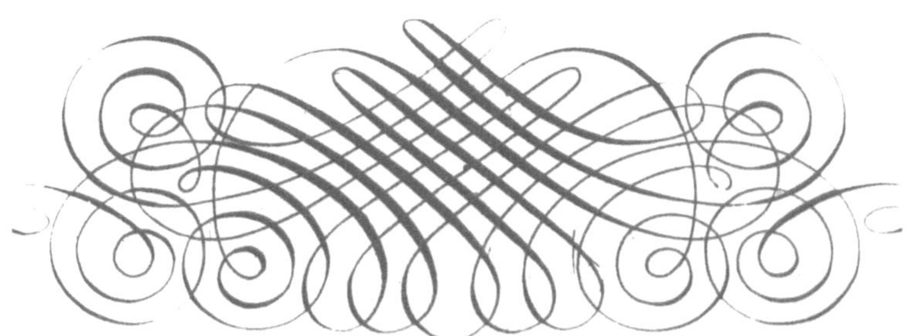

Voice of Liberty

For decades now I'd been home on our all-American soil
As I flew to Dallas for professional conference and found
My biggest education came from the workshops not a bit
But rather, from riding with the cabbies all along the way
For many with accents had sweetest life stories to tell:
A German working hard at the hotel to better himself
Learning to speak English by day, work part time by night
One from Afghanistan arrived to escape political strife
Speaking poignantly of home now part of a past long ago
An Indian finally could live away from castes to limit him
A British black had prayers to raise his daughter well
And a Nigerian was proud to drive to control his own destiny
In three short days our country had become precious again
As I heard these men tell of opportunity offered the world
And was touched to hear strangers speak with such passion
How they valued their freedom and loved their new land!
What those workshops had been about no longer can I recall
But memory of the Voice of Liberty still rings clear in my head

On Youth

Que Sera

Que sera?
I face my life and open my arms to the unknown
I seek
What shall I find?
I dream
What shall I become?
I think
What shall my ideas reap?
I am but a girl with fierce desires and fervent ambitions
No.
I am a girl, but with fierce desires and fervent ambitions
There is a difference.
Shall I be a woman who never did
      what her girlhood beckoned?
Que sera?
The challenge is there
You say I cannot.
Why?
Just because you never did?

ON WOMEN

Who I Am

For so many years I tried to decide
Who I am
Deep down I've known
But no one else did
I aim to please the family
But doing so often doesn't give me
The sense of self that I really need
For me to be true to me
The men in my life love football
And concrete things, you see
They hardly know I'm not of their world
Even though I try to be
What I love is as different
As womanhood is from them
There's art and
        there's poetry and
                there're feelings and
                        there's Communication

Self Portrait

The idea of the road not taken means so much to me
For at times I feel as if I live an uncommon life
Woman without women, colleague without peer
Devoted to cooking, having no other domestic desire
Searching for understanding of a lone point of view
In my own household full of human and feline males
Henbird believing in classic difference, independence
Praying not to smother the one who's leaving the nest
So he may return to me not having been held too tight
Treasuring streak of spirit in the happy little one
At times wondering if either of them loves me for me
Asking for freedom within a concept of family unity
Raising the boys to respect the views of womankind
Trying to teach them both of equality, democracy
So that when they each have lived to reach my age
They will have learned to truly accept their wives
Whose opinions would be valued as much as their own

Pathfinder

There was a time you were close and together
Though now he is figuratively or literally dead
So you struggle for the strength to carry on
Managing to control fear except in your dreams
To find that none gave you credit for survival
And none may have encouraged you to succeed
Or you may have wondered, twenty years later, why
Only men went to college to study subjects
You now are convinced you, too, would have loved
Awaken to realize you now must fight for identity
And a rightful place in society where you belong
As a contributor, a nurturer, a pathfinder
A woman whose greatest discovery is learning
How wonderful she can be just having faith in herself

I Had No Shoes

I woke feeling somewhat sorry for myself
Still unpleased to face another surgery
And meet inconvenience again so soon
Then all of us dressed and went to church
With me wearing a coat of self-consciousness
Heavy in the sense I failed to look my best
I saw a girl there who never stood nor sang-
Betrayed by my body as we were ushered out
I wondered would the minister notice me amiss
From transept an old friend waved hello and hugged
Asking how we'd been, gushing on of grandbe'be'
Then she told me how her lovely daughter's leg
And heel were crushed to bits by wayward car, and
How she'd never, ever, be quite the same again
Now I knew the unsung girl seated across the way
Had been the daughter of my friend, the one
Seen leaving slowly on brace and crutch

All day I've been foolishly ashamed of vanity
Recalling words repeated by my daddy long ago
I cried because I had no shoes
'Til I met a man who had no feet

On Men

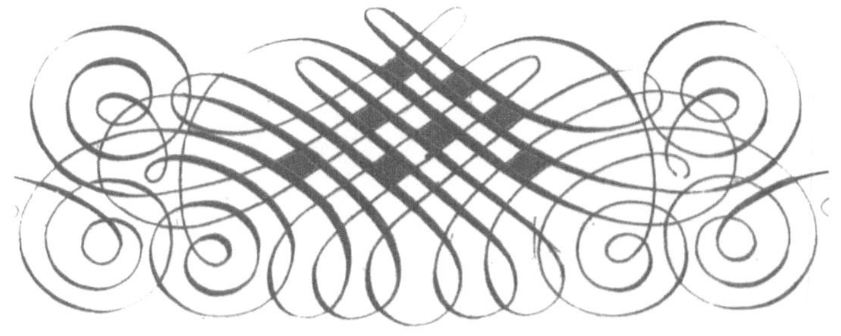

Not Just Me

He walked into my heart singing
And together we walked a while
We sat and talked as I
Dreamed when he sang to me

He walked into my heart smiling
And together we walked a while
We sat and talked as I
Dreamed when he smiled at me

Now I can dream again
With his smile fresh on my mind
But, I can forget the dreams
The power in only the first two bars
Brings a shiver to my spine
But I cannot forget the song
For now its melody's for everyone
Not just me

Ever Blended

You claim I'm the one
Asking you to change...
No, follow your patterns
They don't bother me
What's quietly nagging you
Is that part of yourself
Wondering if it's worth the risk
To finally lay down your sword and
Remove armor shielding your heart
What you don't understand is
All that I want of you is
Everything you already are
Just as long as you begin
To see and accept my strength
Ever blended with sensitivity
I'd readily dare you to return
To familiar comfort zones you knew
If opportunity would be there
From now unto eternity
For the future to bring you
Another woman quite like me

Patience

It seems that patience is a virtue always forced on me
It's reached by circumstance more than my own plan
Where you're concerned it comes if schedules change
For more essential bookings to keep you far from me
There's your nature, proceeding on with no remark
Why say how I feel for you to beg to silence me?

Yet I walk for miles each week allowing vivid memories
Of your voice and touch to fill me up each time
And at half past six last night, oddly I just called
Then hung up the phone, realizing all I had to share
Were forbidden words I couldn't bring myself to say
Aching deep inside for what might have been with you

Rhythm of the Blues

Sounds led us to the past
As you finally rose to take my hand
Leading me to more than dance
Lost in what was seventeen

A lot of time passed by
Before magic in the music
Could capture you again
And beckon you on to me

Standing, smiling, waiting
You finally saw me with your eyes
When I walked through Mona Lisa to
Night of rhythm of the blues

Now instead of once or twice
You danced with me each time
Heart not about to breakthrough
Your distance and hesitation

Then a saxophone man did play
A nocturne song so full and fine
You rescued me with all your soul
As we melted through the floor

Let your dear New Orleans keep
Her voodoo hold on you, and me, for
Music makes us dream again with
Expectation of what's forgotten
        Ecstasy

I Know People

I saw posture, tall, lean, maybe military
He caught my eye all right
I've seen plenty of soldiers and sailors in my time
Macho guy, gruff, walked me to my car
Pure cop. His magic words: I know people
After what I grew up with
He's not even close to being like my dad
Epitome of the tough old bird
My detective honey grilled me day one
Like prime witness to a homicide
Inevitable victim of harsh and fickle mood
Maybe I've been murdered over a span of time
Embracing St. Francis in my wounded mind
Not so much seeking to be understood
As to understand
Giving
That I might break through and eventually receive
As years pass by I wonder
Why I wasted my patience and precious time
Silence is hardly golden when its origin
Is fear and cowardice
He loses grasp on so called masculinity
Claiming most people succumb to feelings
But he doesn't
Stunned, some days he sounds like my father
In his twisted logic and thoughtlessness

The only man I've ever met that reminded me
In studying both
At least my father was a genuine hero
With lifelong history of honesty
And brutal truth
Yet my armed robbery specimen
Betrayed his insistence on trust at the start
Never to be remotely earned
Not bothering to comprehend
The valor of keeping one's word
Plain reliability has been absent
Along with presents and promises
Not a penny's worth on either count
I grieve the person I dreamed him to be
Is neither officer nor gentleman
One Saturday morning he lamented to me
If you were out looking for a guy
I wouldn't be the kind of man you'd pick out
Since I've been informed he is never wrong
Turns out he was right about that as well
I saw in him the man he could become
Instead I found the man he always was

Sweet Is Thy Smile

Sweet is thy smile, like a carefree summer's day
Quick and determined is thy gait
Where doth thou goest?
Thine eyes art blue
But deep and distant art the truths within them
What do they reveal?
Thou art strong; thy breast has courage
Thy heart beats rhythmically, confidently
What doth it feel?
Yes, sweet is thy smile of summer
But summer's days are altered
By swift winds and chilling rains
Wilt thy smile deceive, like thine eyes and heart?
Those drops of rain art my tears, my life blood
For I believe thou art a summer's day
Thou art warm, attentive for a fleeting second
But, in the next, eager to be free and wild
As the teasing winds on a rained-upon distant sea
Winds cannot calm a turbulent heart
Those cruel winds deaden and freeze a soul
The poisonous drops of rain
Transform my soul to useless remembering
Remembering ice
The deathly rains have frozen and imprisoned
Within its walls of memories a passion for thee
My precious one summer morn

Soon

Nice guy nice time
Goodnight
I'll call you soon
Sounds hopeful
Nice guy really nice time
Monday morning too soon
Monday night maybe
Perhaps Tuesday afternoon
Tuesday night
Before supper on Wednesday
Thursday morning maybe
Thursday night's good
Maybe Friday by noon
Early Friday evening
Oh.

So what does soon mean?
How soon is soon?
Does soon mean later?
Does soon mean maybe?
Does soon mean never?

On Love

Is This Love?

Is love praying for you to speak my name?
Is love being happy when you are happy?
Is love tingling when you touch my hand?
Is love crying because I never hear you call?
Crying because you seldom look?
Crying because a touch is rare?
Crying as you notice someone else?
Dying because you don't love me?
Maybe it is love
But is love always so damnably difficult?

If I Knew Once More

Sometimes listening to you is distressing to me
I'm told of those all around who love you so
Who are close by to see and comfort you each day
Friends seem dearer each time I hear about them
So I wonder if, or where, I fit into your life
I'm many miles away, seldom part of your world
Lacking faith to believe my memory stays alive
Once there were touching poems and letters sent
Wrapping me tight with your tender thoughts of me
As I lie here in meditation it seems too long ago
I'm not courageous enough to endure an elusive you
I recall you to say writing only brings you pain
Yet words are all I have to hold in my hand
To remind me I've a special place in your heart
Polite little notes could be sent to just anyone
Maybe I need more than you're willing to give
I'd trade any bauble for prized poetry or prose
If I knew once more I belong somewhere in your soul

Letters in My Head

In the stillness between the storms of my life
I have time to be aware of a fullness overflowing
While I hide my thoughts to keep you feeling safe
As if what's left unsaid is somehow less true
Dinners with you are in my imagination
Dances with you are in my dreams
Letters to you are in my head
Presents to you are in my heart
I'm learning to be close but not inseparable
To be caring...but not care
To be giving...but not give
To be loving...but not love

If Only

Today I stand to watch the door
She entered once
I wish that I had known
She loved me
I think back on the morns
She smiled on
I wish that I had known
She loved me
To recall the flowered fragrance
She smelled of
I wish that I had known
She loved me
So often in her bedroom
She cried so
I wish that I had known
She loved me
And my blind eyes now see
She suffered there
I wish that I had known
She loved me
No, I only wish now she had known
I loved her

If You Loved Me

If you loved me, I'd be eternally happy
If you loved me, the depth of emotion
In your serene eyes would tell me
If you loved me, the world would be ever
Illumined in gold, scented in rose
If you loved me, the celestial bodies
Would bless us as they'd laugh joyously
Twinkling and peeking at their children
If you loved me, each word uttered
Would praise peace and harmony
If you loved me, I would be dwelling
In paradise, pleased with my role as thine

But you don't love me and will never
My would be's will never be, ever
And my jubilant heart, which would
Have sung hymns of joy, songs of cheer
Will not be heard- never heard
For no sound emanates from a broken soul

And Love

They sat and ate and drank
Told dirty jokes and swore
They worked and cleaned
And spent money
And loved
They fought hard and sweat
Sang songs and prayed
They gambled and sewed buttons
And read books
And loved
They saw movies and plays
Gossiped and blackmailed
They cried and laughed
Trusted little
And loved
They were confident and afraid
Lived carefully and dared
They did everything
And as an afterthought
They loved
But even so all was done
For love

Cry, Cry, Cry

Cry, cry, cry
But cry so silently
For none should see the bitter tears
Deep in the heart of me
Cry, cry, cry
For our love, it's so shattered, dead
The cruel truth and lonely sadness
Wing quickly to my head
Cry, cry, cry
But cry so patiently
For yet another day shall dawn
To remind myself of thee
Cry, cry, cry
And then cry no more
The memory of the pain and you
Are locked forever more
Cry, cry, cry
And pray that hour will come
When all those tears are forgot
And the final years are some
Cry, cry, cry
For the youth, spent and sweet
It strengthened my innocent soul
And the fierce desire to meet
Cry, cry, cry
For he shall escape me never

Times we spent I know and love
I am to be haunted forever
Cry, cry, cry, cr

Sayonara, Au Revoir, Arrivederci

My love, to fall in love, I didn't mean
For now, how can I ever part
After the plenty I will see the lean
And with it, your broken heart
I meant to tell you of my going
But my lips froze from the start
A sayonara t'your eyes aglowing
Would stab their brilliance like a dart
I go, my love, for I'm not free
Although I've often prayed to stay
I'm but a silly coward, love, you see
And au revoir seems to be the only way
So I walk from behind my many lies
Mouthing arrivederci with my silent eyes

The Welcoming

I was reminded of an empath creature who came from light years away
With senses so keen she embodied the emotion of mankind
Radiating eternal love, absorbing suffering of the centuries
As he gently whispered open when deep inside me
At that moment I understood he knew me better than I know myself
As reservation evaporated with acceptance as my state of mind
The welcoming was the brightest ball of white light
Surrounding me with generations of warmth and love
A oneness of our joining without beginning and without end
A union the least of which involved our earthly bodies
Same mind and heart, same soul and spirit
Taking us beyond the limits of space and time and substance
To newborn dimensions unknown in this primitive world
To a place where Thought lives on as our immortality

Worship

It says to have
No other gods before me
So why am I worshiping
Someone of this earth
Someone of the flesh?
This is the one in whose arms
I finally feel cherished and adored
For the very first time
Has this man become
Flesh to dwell among us?
I have been preparing
My table before him
For the longest part of my life
Becoming the woman
In whom he could trust
When Divine intervention
Would bring us together
Learning through temptation
And trespasses
The pain of living
Through relationships
Dying time after time
Learning to reach
A plateau of acceptance
Of my strengths
And many frailties

Learning to love boundlessly
Within fear of loss and departure
Facing both too many times to count
I believe he was sent to me
On a mission from God
To teach my soul of peace
And unconditional love
Things I had only dreamed of
For so many years
I began to doubt and lose faith
Yet God has heard me
Through years of spoken
And unspoken hopes and prayers
A lifetime of sensing
What I was born for
Generations of frustration
As no one understands me
An endless battle fought
Terrified of never
Finding my dream
He is a man who is
Goodness incarnate
Loving another as he
Would want to be loved
Generously giving without
Expectation of return
Joyfully sacrificing
To protect and to keep me
Now he is here for me

Yes, a beauty and a god
A man of all my realities
A man for all my seasons
A man of all my prayers
And so, yes, Lord,
I do worship him

Offering Salvation

His voice melodious as psalms
Memorable as scripture
His eyes of the Sistine
Sheer purity and peace
Fine nose brushing my cheek
A hallowed experience
Warmth of his breath
A whisper from heaven
His tongue touching me
Rhythmic as morning prayer
Fingers as gossamer
Bring quivers of rapture
His body's softness
A cape of spiritual warmth
His hands underneath me
Offering salvation
Under his weight
I am transfigured
The gentle depth of his love
Moments of kingdom come

On Marriage

Clairvoyance Never's Worn by Brides

Never did I as a young girl believe
There'd be such complication to life
First I'd study and then I'd marry
Planning to live life happily ever after

More than twenty years ago I stood at altar
Imagining what all the years would bring
I couldn't know then the changes I'd see
In pathway and arterial turns, since
Clairvoyance never's worn by brides

Day by day lessons were learned
To forget fantasy of an American dream
Life's not remotely like childhood's longings
It's defined by brambles as much as by blossoms

Serenity born of disappointment
Tolerance born of injustice
Compassion born of suffering
Acceptance born of anguish
Happiness born of pain

Laughter's worthless without the tears
And success is empty without the struggle
While the best things in life are free
What's most precious comes at heaviest price

I'd map all my future as best I could
But planning applies only in financial doings
In emotional matters we're far better served
To patiently wait and greet every year
Welcoming our days simply one by one
Trusting finer instincts of the heart
To right calculated wrongs of the mind
Every decided and faulty step of the way

Eventually time will tell the answers
For all that's truly meant to be
Computation of life's equation
Is achieved through abiding faith, and
Reducing every argument to simply say

In the end all that ever matters
Is whether there is Love

Notes on Why I Married You

Watching you walk
Across the dance floor
I found you irresistible
So tall, strong, all American
Honest face
Kindest eyes
Warmest voice
Solid as a rock
Always reliable
Always on time
No flash
All substance

The first two weeks
You spent all your IRS refund
On surgery for Duch
I knew anyone who loved animals like that
Was someone for me

Then you gave a shirt to my boy
On his birthday
The same month we began seeing each other
No one else
Had ever cared for my son
I first fell in love with you
For the way you cared about me
Through my young son

Within the first three months
I was sure of you
Praying this fine man
Would love me, too
You were what I wanted
I saw something in you
No one else did
All the depth and goodness
All the possibilities
All of my future
Wrapped up in this quiet Texan
Full of tender mercies

Today
You still are
All the possibilities
All of my future

How I love you

Great Expectations

Lament that I have great expectations of you
As if goals and standards are set too high
Yet you don't realize I never expect too much
Of those who cannot do or simply cannot be
Only those whose capacity seems to be there
Begging for me to bring it out and share
My finest gift is perceiving personalities
Having intuition to know if potential's near
I always believe in still waters running deep
And relied on maturity to make you understand
None has ever believed in you more than I do
And none other would ever hope so long to see
Blossoming of love and companionship so real
And so priceless to be truly worth the wait

Now When I Leave

So long ago I tried to explain that no one
Could ever cause me to lose you but you
Doubts were born right within this house
So I fought to maintain the good that was
And to recover hope so quietly about to die
These recent times have been glorious gifts
With wonderful ribbons and bows of happiness
Hours of loving and sharing and giving
Believing and listening and becoming
Precious moments prayed for over time
And imagined often in my sweetest dreams
Whenever I now leave for a day or two
I'll find the joy of growth and of space
Feeling that freedom has been granted
With deepest love of my need to be me
And I leave with the firmest resolve
That even though I need and want to go
I'll do so with determination to return
To the strength and foundation of my life
To hearth and home, to the treasures of you

Founded on Faith

Why don't they tell you that when you begin to feel
You have to face the pain and shed the tears
For a decade of loving without truly being loved
Building on a structure too full of barriers
Seeing all else in life granted greater priority
Wanting comfort but finding denial, disappearance
Sharing emotion with measured morsels returned
Having gifts of the heart called monologues
Hearing irritation confiding in strength of self
Being listened to without really being heard
Seeking support with impatience as the prize
Needing approval with criticism as the answer
Craving acceptance, respect, to be ridiculed
Finally so full of hurt the years of pain came
Spilling over and over and over and over
With weeks and months of tears and grief
Reliving memories of every single sadness
Acknowledging truths so very hard to admit
Yet waiting for the moment of redemption
Where bitterness, anger and anguish may be gone
Praying for resurrection to come and reveal
A depth of love still there which cannot die
Founded on faith in a diamond in the rough

How to Handle Sand

The needlepoint is one of my favorites
For saying if you love something
Then set it free
If it comes back, it is yours
If it doesn't, it never was
This lesson would be your greatest gift to me
To learn all about balance and reciprocity
To have held me loosely in the palm of your hand
Like grains of sand upon the beach's shore
Because if you try to hold the sand too tight
Surely will it slip right through your fingertips
Yet if you hold it gently with an open hand
An entire cup of priceless sand will stay

My Rock and My Comfort

Through the years he has been my rock and my comfort
As I've lived each day of my life to please him entirely
Thoroughly planning my activities around his wants and wishes
And staying home with babies when both boys were so young
As I grew older I found I had nurtured them all but myself
With tears marking time from early married to middle age
So I am learning to write for my soul and walk for my spirit
And spread love through my life for those who will See me
Never intending to leave the men of my family out of my life
But rather just asking them to accept me for being myself
To let me cultivate my own interests and build my own peace
A feminine part of them whose needs are both different and the same
The strongest love lives on but with woman's definition
Just emphasizing my own right to be considered equally
Praying for understanding and justice among unintended male domination
Never having realized 'til now how my self had been left behind
So I beg my rock and my comfort to kiss and hold me tight
And still choose to live with this butterfly flown from cocoon

On Children

Nighty-night, Sleep Tight

From six months on, my little son went nighty-night
Hearing fairy tale stories one after the other
With books becoming his windows of the world
Wondrous to behold every moment he drew breath

Then, sleep tight, don't let the bedbugs bite
Amid the Our Father, now I lay me down to sleep
After showers of many kisses, rainbows of many hugs
With heavy-lidded eyes and beebees held dear
His blankets to guard his body 'til the dawn
Wee angel would fly away with a Sand Man

Now years have passed and babe is become boy
How do I lie there not falling asleep hearing sobs
Over beebees now carefully hidden, gone far away?
And how do I steal security away from a child
When through the years I've gradually come to know
Men are still the same as their little boys?

Only difference is the daddies have learned so well
To hide truth of their preference to stay Peter Pans
But sons will cry out in honest desperation
They simply never want to grow up

Golden Boy

Five months before you were born
I had already named you
There was never any doubt
That you would become what you are
First in our lives, first in our hearts, and much beloved
This very definition embedded in your name
Every day of your life
I smiled when you said you didn't like your name
Since I knew what you did not
That many have said what a fine name you had
Symbolic and beautiful and masculine and strong
Just as you are
My first splendid accomplishment
My sunlit son of whom I am most proud

I admire you for the exceptional qualities you possess
God blessed you with a wonderful capacity
To think and to feel
The greatest parts of you still untapped
As you leave to begin your life
Abilities of leadership and discipline
And perseverance to be tested
Keenest mind and memory, heart laden with gold
A generosity of spirit to glory
In the achievements of your friends
Never to envy or belittle others who were recognized

Having confidence and humility enough
To believe that knowledge of your own performance
Of magic and excellence is well enough
Many a time others have been too jealous
To acknowledge talents so rare
They're criticized being effortlessly shown
Having a joy of life to lead each day
With laughter and with energy
To value most the sure and constant love
Of teammates, friends and family
Never smitten by superficiality or appearance
But with the plainest of reality
Being quiet in your faith in God
Without show or outward display
Never caring about whom to impress
But how to find sheer happiness
Always enamored of life so much
That time has little meaning

On Death

Memories of Mammaw

I look around our house and find
Afghans everywhere to wrap up in
All made with perfect stitches
And each one made of love

Feisty and so strong she was
Honest through and through
I was proud that she took to me
Hugging me hard at each hello
Patting me hard at each goodbye
As if I were born into family

I will never forget that eventful day
My first one seeing a becoming side of death
Friends she'd known seventy of ninety years
Told wonderful stories, sounding serene
And even quite pleased about how she died

To have given Christmas gifts away a month ahead
To have gussied up for church in all her finery
To have gone to lunch with her dear lady friends
To have lived independently up to final breath
Never becoming a burden to her family or society
How like her to have probably planned it all!

Amid many tears there was joyous laughter
As a community gathered 'round to say goodbye
We admired her in splash of color, floral display
Bound together for festive funeral, unlike others
Celebration being part of a long and healthy life

Yet I noticed as she lay there, oh so lovely
Such a difference in the way she looked that day
She seemed but a shell of all she used to be
What I saw was body to have merely housed her spirit
Which had traveled far and wide in those three days
To be living on, and lingering still among us
As we passed her by in silent fare thee well

Rite of Passage

Was this the man who suffered almost fifty years ago?
Were there times he thought he'd never see home again?
Were there times he would feel Taos nearby as he awoke?
Were there dreams he would have a glorious son someday?

The two of you were alone together
As he chose the time to drift away
Maybe it was meant to be like this
For father and son to be side by side
At the departure

Did he see the tiny baby boy you once were?
Did he see you in his arms and hear you cry?
Did he kiss scraped knees and hold you tight?
Did he watch you grow from boy into finest man?
Did he cherish your own babies as they came along?
Did he share the joy hearing of your accomplishments?
Did he tell you that you mattered more than life itself?

Aftermath

They wept when she was losing weight and fighting stomach pains
They wept when she became depressed and no one really knew it
They wept when she turned to drugs after months of feeling bad
They wept when she walked nearby giving picture books away
They wept when she left behind her mother, sons and husband
They wept for potential lost as two failed to find themselves again
They wept for senseless tragedy, endless suffering, as ones endure
Hours days weeks months and zombied years have now passed
As aftermath flows along while I too weep blood rivers of tears
Hearing of a comely and dear woman unable to bear her burdens
Feeling mountains of sorrow for helpless ones who found her
Knowing I never would've met the precious man to tell her story
Hadn't she gone to a closet with a Magnum 357 held to her head

Sleep

Golden curls fall on your brow
Hush, now, don't you cry
Sleep, my precious, sweetly now
And close your big blue eye

Pinks flushed your chubby cheek
And happy laughter filled the air
I knew 'twas all so bleak
To glance and see you there

God himself is in your face
So pure, my doll, art thou
Though I quickly lose my race
I press you to me now

Your tiny hands pull at my hair
This morn so bright and clear
I'd kiss your nose, if I'd dare
But that's too hard I fear

Close your eyes, my little one
Hush, now, don't you cry
The race of Sleep is run, and won
And makes your Mama die

Laugh

She laughed at me, oh, how she laughed
So freely and so free
Her voice like gales of winter wind
Tore my heart from me
How lovely did she smile that time
In her pleasant, laughing way
Until I smiled and took her lips
Which shall not laugh today

When I Died

Heather lost its color
Roses failed to bloom
Trees shriveled and folded
Blades of grass collapsed
Butterflies, bees buzzed no more
Birds forgot to fly
When I died
And the rivers turned to ice
Rocks split in half
The ground became blue carpet
Cliffs cried out in pain
There were laughs and sighs no more
Seas ceased to roll
When I died
As does everything, I died
And just me, just me, and my dead domain
Know of the one less speck
Of light tonight

On Parents

Preface

A relationship with a mother and daughter is not always perfect. Ambivalence is not unusual. Mother was always a housewife except for the first year of her marriage. When I was a young girl I would sometimes come home from school and find two new outfits laid out on my bed. My mother would have bought them that day. Finding clothes on my bed was a treat, because normally my mother made all my clothes. She chose the patterns, she chose the colors, and showed me dresses after she had finished making them. Those were the clothes I wore. Later I wondered if she loved me best when I was her little girl, like a doll she could dress up any way she liked. When I went away to college at seventeen, never to return to my parents' home except for holidays, I began to find her resentful of me. Once I was independent, self-reliant, and confident in my adult life, she treated me differently. She seemed to be angry that I was working and would ask now and then, "When are you going to quit your job?" I would answer, "Mama, I'm not planning to quit my job. I plan to retire." I knew that what she really meant was that she missed me. She hoped I would come home. I missed her, too, but my life and my job were far away. When Mother was only nineteen, she had traveled across the world by herself to join my father in the Army. She ran the household and took care of the family alone when my father was overseas for more than a year at a time. Frequently she took care of the household for six weeks to two months while Dad was on maneuvers. She moved children across the seas by herself and bought a house and a car.

Her own family was never nearby to help her. Looking back on those years, I see a strong Army wife who never complained and never cried. Especially after I was grown, communicating with my mother was like walking on eggshells. I was incredibly adept to avoid the landmines because I knew her so well. Phone calls and visits were both wonderful and excruciating. In the pleasant moments, I would say to Mother, "I wish you would quit smoking." She would say, "The doctor didn't tell me to quit smoking." I would say, "But, Mama, the doctor does not love you." About fifteen years after this routine first began, Mother called me very excited to tell me she had quit smoking. I was thrilled for her and told her how happy I was to hear it. Unfortunately, a few months later she was diagnosed with severe breathing difficulties and a greatly enlarged heart. For a couple years she was housebound, and then later, she was bedbound. During one of my visits, we sat on the front porch having a good talk, and Mother asked me, a bit exasperated, "What is it you want?" I answered, "All I want is for you to love me. Just love me." The last year we had together was very comfortable, finally. When she was in the hospital again, with my father and brother unconcerned about her condition, I spoke to her over the phone long distance. On a Friday night, I called the hospital again to speak to Mother, and we spoke just a moment, and then she began to say to me over and over and over and over and over, "I love you, I love you, I love you, I love you, I love you, I love you, I love you...." in a soft, faraway voice that faded to a whisper. I could not speak. The next day I called the hospital. The nurse told me in an upbeat voice, "She's having a good day. She's been talking about you. She told me, 'I bet she'll be getting on a plane!'" "Oh, dear God," I said to the nurse as I hung up. Instantly I called an airline and raced to the airport. I arrived at the hospital one hour too late.

A relationship with a father and daughter is not always perfect. Ambivalence is not unusual. My father was all military: gruff, tough, harsh, opinionated. At my parents' house there was a photograph of my father in fatigues in Vietnam as an Artillery battalion commander. My mother and I lovingly referred to this picture as "Old Blood and Guts." Since he spent most of his life with soldiers, Daddy knew little about women and even less about daughters. It was not easy to live under his roof. He was Victorian with the conviction that children should be seen but not heard. He spanked hard with a belt in those years when parents spanked children for their transgressions, such as not coming home by dark when playing in the neighborhood. When I was a child he exposed me to art and sculpture and cathedrals when we traveled through Europe. He taught me, "Think before you speak." Daddy would also bark at me, "Why say you're doing right? I only need to tell you if you're doing wrong." In my entire life, my father never once told me if I were pretty. It was many years before I realized that when he said, "Rosalyn, I never had to worry about you," that it was the greatest compliment I would ever receive. Dad was not a gift giver. When I was a teenager I saw my mother cry on her birthday because my dad hadn't given her a card or present. Dad's response to Mother was, "Why cry about one day? What's important is that I'm good to you on all the other three hundred sixty-four." Then Mother would forgive him and partly agree with his logic. The same thing happened every anniversary: no flowers or presents. I had learned Mother was sentimental about gardenias since they were all over her parents' home the day she and Dad married. Dad mellowed as the years passed. On my parents' fortieth anniversary, my father had a florist deliver forty separate gardenia corsages to my mother. During Mother's last three years, my father sat by the phone all day long so he could pick up on the first ring to keep Mother's sleep from being disturbed. Dad only left the house for fifteen minutes every several days to run for groceries, prescriptions, or gas. He cared for Mother with the greatest devotion. After Mother died, my father finally started talking to me. Until then Mother had been intermediary; he would tell her, and then she would tell me. When Daddy was in his eighties, he started to send me one sentence letters in pencil on lined steno pad paper. In each one he told me how proud of me he had always been. I treasure his notes as the presents I had longed for all my life. My father rarely spoke of war, but he gave me a box of Army keepsakes to pass along to my children which include two Silver Stars (that is, one with Oak Leaf Cluster) awarded in Korea and one Bronze Star awarded in Vietnam. Retired as a Colonel with thirty years' service, my father is buried at a national cemetery with his gravestone bearing his name, rank, dates of birth and death, and the following words: World War II, Korea, Vietnam.

I wrote "Flood of Feelings" more than twenty-five years ago. All of it is painful, and all of it is true. Yet the years bring perspective and peace. Each of us is multi-dimensional: both complex and simple, good and bad. And in the end, all that ever matters is whether there is love.

Flood of Feelings

Stop, I said
Don't do this to me
There is so much you don't know
One thing I can't stand
Is to hear you criticize
Telling me I must call
Saying don't ask them to love me back
Don't expect reciprocity
I listened to you softly chastise me
In the same tone I have heard before
With that inevitable sound
Of blame being placed on me
As if somehow once again it must be
The daughter who's in the wrong
So, no wonder I cried to say
This is one thing I will not allow
There is so much you don't know

Strong as I am
Even I must have time
To be allowed to heal from hurt
Before walking into hurt again
Lately it's been too much

We fought the hurricane
Its trauma and devastation

Grateful to survive
There's one now away from me
Already twice in hospital
And little one in tears of pain
From headaches and the fever
And one is loving me
With anguish and with heart
Taking both breath and bitterness away
And oldest friend I kissed
Saying I love you so
Your life has value
Begging her not to go
So far away from us
Where none would see
More marks and bruises
Scarring her precious body
Where none would know to ask, as I did
If she would ever be all right
And the worries over work
That never seem to end
Then there's you and suffering family
And fear for your father
Frail and weak and fading
So little I can do
As life gently passes by

It's not time yet
Don't speak to me today
There's so much left to say

Another time
There's so much you don't know

What you don't know
Is that contacting them at all
Brings such miserable pain
Frustration, sadness, tears
Calling them at night
Causes loss of sleep
Calling them at day
Knots my stomach tight
It's never satisfactory
I need fullest strength
To be willing to cope at all
In anticipation of the
Grim blackness

The wise lady asked years ago
How do you feel right now?
I feel so very
Bad

Do you realize your whole face
Dropped
With infinite sadness
Being reminded of them?

How did you feel when you went there?
Wary, apprehensive, tense, reserved

Unlike myself
But like I was
When I lived in their house

But I was happy
In class at school
With teachers and classmates
Who encouraged and supported me
How did you feel driving away?
Joyous, relieved, grateful to be gone

So forgive what they've become
Objectively face what they are
Ones who hurt your very health
Without truly meaning to
You do the best you can
Move on from your inner child
Be proud of who you are
Distance yourself from them
Be aware of the limits
And find what good is left
Those who bring us to this world
Sometimes have dragons of their own
They repeat the same mistakes
Long ago made with them
Go on with life
With your head held high
For the loss is theirs

I'm so tired today
I cannot face
Criticism
Ridicule
Disappointment
Disapproval
Regret
Their wishing I could be
Something I am not
Something I have never been

I was the flawless daughter
Always obedient
Never rebellious
Perfect student
Honoring father and mother
Even through my tears
Of loneliness and deepest sadness
Living in the shadow of favored brother
Told to let him have his way

Showing term papers and poems
Never to be read
Always too busy for me
Being recognized at schools
Year after year after year
With him never caring to go
Graduating twice

At the very, very top
With neither of them
Even there

I would ask her to listen
Asking for fairness
Wondering why he never talked to me
And why I couldn't go
Why nothing I ever did or said
Brought me any praise
Yet the fault was always mine
I shouldn't be asking why

Years of being alone
Moving across the seas
No friends my age for
Months at a time

Permission granted to go
Nowhere
Tears in my room
When I couldn't go
Robbed of my youth
I lived in books and poetry
I did not select solitude
It was all I had

I accepted life as best I could
Without acknowledging what I was

Surprised
I heard him say to me
You're the saddest girl I ever met
Hindsight tells me
It was true
In pictures now I see the girl I was
Blossoming quietly
But those eyes
Cause me to grieve
For me

I guess we'll keep you another six months
You only made A's because you're his pet
I don't need to tell you when you're right
Only when you're wrong
(So I'm always wrong?)
Your major isn't good enough
For you there's fabric seconds
You're not worth roses
(I asked for so little)
It's all behind you now
(Remark for the honor graduate?)
The ring's for you
With disappointment in her voice
You're just what she'd wanted
She'd be so proud
(Why weren't you proud, too?)
Mothers who work don't really love their children
(That can't be true?)

When are you going to quit your job?
(Never)
You don't need that nice a house
(Why not?)
There's money for brother's trip to Australia
(But not for me?)
Yelling over the phone
We won't come to your wedding
You deliberately tried to exclude us
(What paranoia is this?
I do not understand
I do not understand)
Their boycotts of rehearsal dinner
And wedding breakfast
(Such a loving family
Such a haunting memory)
She refuses to talk to you
You're not welcome here
You must confess you deliberately mistreated your mother
(I won't say it
I can't say it
It's not true
I never in my entire life
Ever
Deliberately mistreated my mother)
Your hair looks like horse hair
(My hair is golden lovely)
Those glasses don't become you
(I chose them myself, for my own face)

I feel so sorry for your son
He's such a pathetic little orphan
(This happiest child that ever was?
He's lucky to have two fathers dearly love him
But even if they dropped dead tomorrow
He'd be no orphan
Since I've always been here
Devoted mother
Loving him and caring for him
Every hour of every day of his life)
The hem is much too long
You shouldn't have bought that car
You shouldn't have bought that house
(They don't know what it cost
Or what we make
So why do they say this?)
The workmanship of this house is lousy
(This house?
The most beautiful house
Any of us ever lived in?)
We don't like what you say in your long letters
(I poured hours of thought and care into them
But now I'll stop)
We didn't like you then
(What else is new?)
You called today, why wasn't it yesterday
(But I called when
You would not
It hurts to call)

You visited now, why wasn't it before
(But I visited when
You would not
It hurts to visit)
On my fifty poems given as a present
Are you a pacifist?
(With inference tone, a Communist)
Do you see yourself liberated woman?
(With nauseated tone, disgust)

My questions and my answers
Have been only in my mind
I never argued
Never fought back
Turning the other cheek
Two wrongs don't make a right

We don't like to travel
We don't like the humidity
We don't like your husband

Excuses all

Actually
They don't like me

It took a lifetime to discover
The wrong was not in me
It took a lifetime of endless trying

Of being thoughtful
Of being considerate
Of sending presents
Of writing letters
Of remembering special days
Of never forgetting
In order to fully understand
My countless products of
Excellence
Never
Would ever please

Yet I still try
Never to have given up
Never to have quit
In a lifelong attempt
To overcome the insurmountable
Courageous and mature
To do my part
To be adult in the face
Of childishness, cruelty, injustice
Knowing I will have tried
Unto death
To have struggled so
To reach them

On Friends

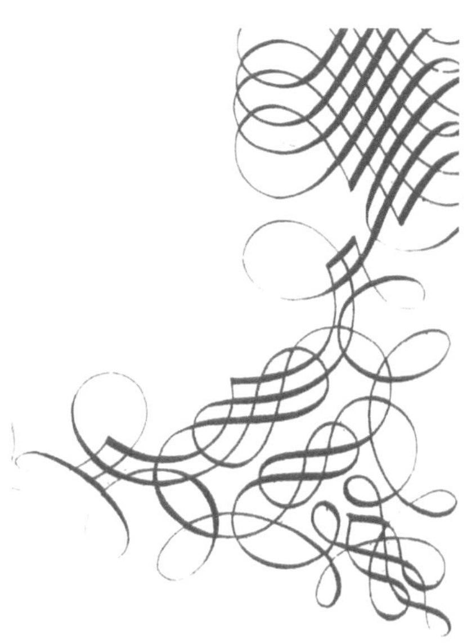

Friend

"Friend" is not a simple word
For a friend is a rare find
Like silver found unexpectedly in the sand
And throughout one's life there are so few
Decades go by and there might be one
If lucky there might be two
A twin of the heart
A kindred spirit
A merge of two mentalities
A relative of the mind far closer than blood

Who's Pudgy, Silly, Sissy?

He said he was pudgy
For having sinking jowl
Spreading waistline
He said he was silly
For returning from Africa
Dancing at dinner on honeymoon
He said he was sissy
For feeding the homeless
Movies making him cry

Yet I met a man
So handsome
Everyone just stares
Who intoxicates all
With his infinite charm
A man whose goodness
Inspires one to prayer
So who is it
Who's pudgy, silly, sissy now?

His Friend

He built a great wall around himself
When he told of his dearest friend
We had scarcely met each other that day
When he deliberately, delicately let me know
His primary purpose in traveling there
Although she never really arrived at all
Her presence was in his every sentence spoken

He let me in a tiny window of his heart
By understanding something of my substance
Through a message seen in my smile
From a distance I listened patiently
To many portraits painted of his friend
It seemed I learned to let her in my life
In order to have him speak to me at all

He finally opened a door around himself
With brushstrokes of me painted in his mind
As our own friendship and many letters grew
Then one darkened day he learned that she had died
Without ever telling him why she'd never flown
And now both of us grieve and love her so
For this precious friend had sent her Love to me
This friend whose name I still don't even know

None Other

He walks into a room without pretense but with regal air
Deliberate, disciplined, standing afar yet among them
He seems alone in his thoughts, a man of fewest words
With influence often so much more than it appears to be
Many believe themselves to know him while they do not
It took years of observation to understand just who he is
I'd hear what seemed a casual remark only to finally appreciate
His awareness had been keen, his phrasing sure and shrewd
His visions of tomorrow grow from a kind and gentle way
To lead by determined example of excellence and good
Dreams of glowing future for poor but unforgotten children
Rest on his faith in families made whole and strong
And his mission lives to encourage and empower everyone
To realize all are blessed with special gifts from God
Of thousands who have crossed my path in a lifetime
I can name none other friend of whom I am more proud
Nor is there anyone in whose word I have more trust
Softspoken man cherished for his constancy and truth

Brave Eagle

All this time they've seen you as silly, simple and common
One whose abilities wouldn't seem memorable to the hereafter
Whose words have never before sounded magically musical
Whose heart would not seem large enough to hold us all
Whose goodness would not seem to bring tears to our eyes
How well I know where the pain in you is coming from
The agony and anguish are coming from within your very soul
The pain is the Truth looking you square in the face
As you grieve that special someones of your daily life
Completely fail to see who you are and what you will be
They can't see thinly spun threads of your sunlit imagination
Or the faintest glimmer of the prince you have become
Surprisingly, right before their dim and clouded eyes

The brilliance of your being's hidden in the shadows of your heart
For eternities of your time twenty-four hours at each stretch
Waiting for a miracle to release you from bondage of tortured soul

You'd be Brave Eagle taking off in full flight
How I long to travel 'neath your expansive wingspan

Bonnie Doone

So long ago I brought her home to me, my five dollar mutt dog
I chose a black bird dog mix from among all the rest for the bond I felt
As she wagged bobbed tail, crooked ears held back
As luck would have it, she became so very sick almost right away
So I nursed her and paid hundreds for a world's worth of care
She turned out to be strong, surviving to surprise me even more
Becoming regal as she grew tall and lean, ebony sleek
For the first few years my dad thought her to be worthless
Sprawled so often in my lap all fifty-five pounds of her
Thinking nothing of climbing on the bed to lie closely nearby
When young, she ran faster than the winds, traveling the miles
To chase fields of birds so far away she couldn't hear me call
How I marveled at the grace and endless speed that took her there!
Finally stories of defending me from harm ensured her value to family
What's more she managed to bring sheer happiness and joy
A combination impossible for us people who vainly do try
I grieved at her fading as she suffered pain so silently
Most would not understand tears from such a sorrowful me
Thinking grief inappropriate for mere dogs like Bonnie Doone
Yet the vet who wept with me sent a cherished sympathy card
As we paid our respects for a life defined by nobility
And the finest character most of us humans only pray to achieve

On Life

The Body of History

Watch history die.
It always does.
Only details, names, and dates still breathe
Truth and poignance are buried with the era
Last remnants begin to pass away
They die with their history
They die unobserved
On the brink of an unfamiliar
      civilization's debut
The old ones sit, silently rocking
Their world is gone
They wait, also to be gone.
They trespass a history they did not create
They are interlopers
Their thoughts are faraway:
They reach the cemetery of the dead Athens
The dead Rome
The dead Carthage
The dead Nineveh
The dead Thebes
The dead Byzantium
The dead glory of the Old South
All are forgotten and gone with the wind
Their truths are pollen caught in the breeze
Pollen is tribute to that which succumbs
It floats over the earth's surface

Going nowhere and recorded by none
The wisdom of history cannot be told
It must be reborn, as truth is relived
The old men think of their past
And knowledge floats unnoticed
Unnoticed like seed across the field
Which quietly is sewn in new furrows
And develops and grows in future eras
History is a skeleton
Its essence deteriorates after time takes the epoch
The true portrait fades
Left behind is only a mere shadow
A reminder of what was
A hint of what will be

Sounds

There is the sound of the wind whistling around a house
And the sound of a city's rush hour
And the sound of a country cricket hum
And the sound of a clock ticking in an empty room
Sounds that fill the mind, that are sounds but to the thinker
And the silent sounds that echo through the woods when only a lone
rabbit hears

There is the sound of a fallen steel pole and hammers
And roosters crowing boldly
There is the sound of tears
The sound of newborn babies shouting their arrival
In the world of sound
The sound of mother crying to see her first born
And the sound of another weeping at her first born's wedding
There is the sound of a strong man crying ashamed, futile tears
And the sound of loved ones at a death bed
When there is no more sound

There is the sound of a grand piano out of tune
And the sounds of violins grabbing hearts in an expectant audience
And the sound of drums beating emotion across the vast wasteland
There is the sound of a lonely guitar strumming
The sound of full choral tones
And the sound of a single scared voice whispering words
The sounds of parties, breaking bottles and drunk laughter

The sounds of parties, breaking bottles and drunk laughter
The sounds of perspiring people rushing to the subway
The sounds of poor kids popping gum
The sounds of a young teacher trying to reach his pupils
The sounds of rosary beads clicking in the hands of a nun
Who has lost her vocation

There are the sounds of understanding
There are the sounds of indifference
There are the sounds of ignorant people asking questions to learn
And the sounds of brothers playing with sisters
There are the sounds of love-hate-jealousy-youth
They are the everyday sounds that pass with maturity
But live on with tomorrow's children

There is the sound of a rocking chair and a kitten purr
There is the sound of pain and agony
And the hopeless sound of beaten nations
When the victorious take their homes and their dignity
There are the sounds of marching boots
And the sound of patriotism at its height
There is the sound of marching boots that swells and fades away
And there is the sound of fear
When the earth vibrates the return of the boots

There is the sound of the sea washing upon the rocks
And the sounds of birds in flight
The call of the gulls
And the flutter of a freezing sparrow's wings

And the sounds of alpine waterfalls in June
The sounds of a tree burning to its roots
And the scampering sound of forest creatures
There is the sound of a wolf growling and tearing flesh
And the sound of a puppy licking one's hand
There is the sound of a cat clawing a prized drapery
And the sound of a vase falling to a marble floor

There is the sound of a scratchy record
And the sound of water dripping in a full bath tub
And the sound of a light switch in the dark
And the sound of gas saturating a hotel room

These are the sounds of Time
For Time is only eternal living, much living
Living makes sounds
And all sounds have meaning

Yet there is no sound to compare
With the sight of two expressive eyes looking desperately into
Your own

Sounds reveal a portion of life
But eyes reveal the depth of the soul
And all of us crave the meaning of the soul
When there is no sound save the heartbeat
In one's own breast

On Time

Starry Heavens

Starry heavens, twinkle on
Into the sleepy night time
(Even keeping watch upon
The shadowed, waking morn)
Dim behind some sunny rays
Humbly forfeiting proud reign
O'er Apollo's Realm of Days
Whimper not, ye saddened stars
Of Sunlight's seeming glory
Men slave and sweat in her heat
But think on thy grand beauty
So, starry heavens, twinkle on
Into the sleepy night time
Lighting, so boldly, darkness yon

Vigil

Upon the break of a new glorious morn
Each flippant wild bird sang in harmony
His approval of the warmth of the golden sun's rays
Soon, the cloak of dew
On the blossoms in the awakening fields
Folded back for the new day
Rodents chattered away as they sought
Appetizing tidbits for breakfasts
The majestic hills in the distance gazed protectively
At the valleys below
The denser brush was there
The fresh scent of forest greenery
Floated in the brisk air
The deer shyly and silently made their way
To the turbulent mountain streams for water
There, a temperamental bear pawed the rapids for fish
Later a few butterflies would flit
From clover to dandelion
Trees cradled the young that napped
Beneath their motherly boughs
Sun peaked out from behind a passing cloud
And marveled at the unblemished land
Dusk arrived too soon
But before the sun would relinquish
Her guardianship for another day
She hesitantly retreated beyond the mountains

And left fiery red and orange streaks on the horizon
As a reminder to the enveloping night
That she would return early on the morrow

Honey Bee

Honey bee, honey bee, of black and gold
Dominate our meadows and steal treasures of succulent honey
First you flew to me
A clover all purple and heavy with sweetness
I reveled in your buzzing about my head
In the late morning hours, flitting to and fro
Winging hum, you sucked my wealth
(and sacked some pollen on the side)
And returned to your ordered kingdom
Yet you came to me always
To my welcome
Day after precious day
Now you have passed me by
My luster has faded with the season
But my loyalty is perennial
Can't you visit me anyway
On your sojourn?
To see you dip and turn and buzz about the meadow
And leave me to my lonely days
Is like an angry sting
Honey bee, you might just as well have stung me
For the same lingering pain is there

Approach

The morn brings pain and heartache
Midday, the host of regret
Afternoon, the harsh reality that is
And dusk, the darkness of despair
Twilight brings the light to shine upon your brow
And the nighttime, the silence to seek your mind
Letting your thoughts feel the morrow
Approaching, as you do

Give to Me a Pleasant, Full Life

Give to me a pleasant, full life
Open heavens flickering a silvery hue
Breezes scented sweet with summer's honeysuckle
The resonant sound of a serious voice
The sleepy night echoing cricket hums
The life of the Present, the natural beauty
May the many memories of the past come
Forth and bring a smile to my wrinkled face
A tear to my aging cheek
May there yet be a future with fulfillment?
There must be a time allotted to me
I shan't survive, cannot, without true purpose
Time, howe'er infinite, must you
Clock away my precious time?
Why my hours? Mine are too short!
Time steals my life away from me
If I do not guard my time wisely
Life shall pass me by
Live, live each minute, each moment, each day
I must gather my memories in bloom
And pluck them daily
Time, give me time
Will I die happy, fulfilled?
Allow me, now, to live my Today
For Today may be the only

The only chance I have
Ah, forgotten Past
Why did I waste my precious time?

On Loneliness

Wait

Until molten rock cooled, Man waited
Patiently for the dawn
After all the infinite darkness
As with my fellow man, I wait
Patiently for the dawn
After all the infinite darkness
But, unlike Man, I shall not wait
So long
Best bring me some dawn
To fight the dark abyss in which I seem to dwell

As I Stood

As I stood, saturated in symphony
He sauntered over silently staring
With soundless syllables, seeking
I stood shoving him some silver
Still seizing a sonata and a psalm
Strains of song separating us
Smiling simply, he stepped aside
As I stood, suddenly stricken
And somehow so sensitively sorry

Luna Is a Pretty Name for Unhappiness

The world is full of love
And compassion
And friendship
And loyalty
So they say
I know better
My world is full of indifference
And omission
And loneliness
And Januses
So I say
My world is my own
And I walk alone
On its face
I am the backside of the moon
Unseen and eternally neglected

Perseverance's Soliloquy

No man is an island
Entire of itself
Not even me
Should apathy die
My clod shall not wash away
Die Apathy
And with your last desperate breath
Watch love come alive
And with it, my budding humanity

Apologies to John Donne

She Dreams

She dreams of a happy, enchanting life
And the wispy sound of a dusty willow
But awakening from her fairy-tale life
All she finds are muffled tears on pillow

Trapped by people in a disinterested town
She wishes for, dreams of blissful happiness
She thinks of home, a familiar sight or sound
Of scenery, of friends—instead: loneliness

No friend, no sunny pasture or cherished 'membrance
Has she here-thoughts are of a past she does recall
As her face shows no expression; her eyes glance
Toward the filmy vision of a voice and call

Until she reaches to touch that joyous home
Lonely, lonely, lonely does she remain
Because, as yet, the path her mind doth roam
Is paved by hopeful dreams and tears of pain

On Cynicism

He Is

He is empty lives and greasy fingernails and futile tears and a milkless
mother with a dying child. And petty gossip. And he is affluence refusing
to observe the unfortunate, and he is the murderer who resents affluence.
He is the opportunist who succeeds while destroying; he is the warrior and
the arguing peacemaker. He feeds his dog and curses his wife. He loves
his pastor and condemns his congregation. He teaches children prejudice
and injustice while mouthing religion. He is nine to five with a ten minute
coffee break. He is ironing clothes and fixing meals and smilingly attend-
ing social functions while thinking, "Go to hell." He is the drunk shunning
education; he covets money and brother's mistress. He is respect for the
dead and apple pie. He is slanted newspapers. He dreams. He is hypocrisy
and sincerity-with-ulterior-motives. He is oblivious to everything but his
selfish, ignorant hide.

His name is Man.

He is rainbows and sunflowers and prickly pears and rain. He is the grass
beneath your feet and the red dirt stained in your shoe. He is love and the
mountain river rushing by. He is the fallen tree you used to climb. He is
the sun that bakes your status-symboled back a golden brown. And distant
and unknown is He. He is always. He is never. He delivers the drunk,
the snob, the catty matron, the starving illegitimate infant. He watches
his lovely world become a human hell. He cries and mourns and suffers
eternal pangs. He hopes, and continues. He offers goodness on the plate
with temptation. He makes individuals what they are but gives them the
choice to decide what they'll be. He becomes the war cry of massacres. He
is worshiped fifty-two days a year, each Sunday. He is palm branches and

generosity and mercy and ashes and glory and savior.

His name is God.

God is God. Man is Man. God is omniscient; Man is fearing. God is alive and living. Man is blind and socially dying.

Never to be one. From the beginning and unto the endlessness of Time, Man shall stray from his God. The eternal abyss widening.

As always, God is God.

Man is Man.

Man cries, "For thine is the kingdom."

God cries, "Make thy kingdom a kingdom. Then mine will be thine."

Amen

Revenge

The dismal shores rested uncertainly

Pensively

Rocks off the beach jutted

      into the sea with reserved dignity

Today the ocean was tumultuous and deadly

The waves fought the rocks

Trying to pull them into the realm

 of endless and

      d

      e

      p

      t

      h

      l

      e

      s

      s

Blue

The clouds hung, pressing

Low

They were black and full

But not with rain

With violence

The wind out at sea built up volume and steadily increased

        the magnitude and force of the waves

Together the winds and seas lunged toward the

Lone unaware sailboat struggling

Helplessly

To avoid the beach rocks

Suddenly

In one instant

The formidable waves, whistling winds, and even the clouds desperately

Attacked

And massacred the boat

Almost immediately, the clouds disappeared

The storming sea subsided

The violent winds became a soft breeze

Nature was satisfied

She remained supreme by killing brutally on impulse

And then

She returned, at will, to her unpretentious image

Of tranquil beauty

Same Hue as the Moonlight

Alone in the blizzard, always alone, he groped along the mushy path. Ever
onward.

To the dim light

    flickering beyond

Among the trees, the cold shrouds of forest green.

On he walked.

Toward the light. Toward warmth.

Toward security. Toward humanity.

Toward kindness.

As he beat upon the cottage door with his ungloved hand, he glimpsed,
ever so faintly, upon the shadow of a slight figure.

A woman.

She opened the door; quite confidently she did.

She heard his pleas.

Then she busily turned, leaving him on the step

As she closed the door to keep the warmth within.

He stood there. He stood.

He felt alone. So alone. As before.

The woman on the inside returned to her knitting

      by the flaming fire.

Presently she thought to herself.

The snow is lovely tonight

With the moon casting silvery shadows on the boughs of the trees.

She smiled.

Such a lovely scene, such a lovely scene

For the coming of Christmas.

Then she thought of her yuletide sacrifice.

Her annual offering, the one she had been preparing this evening.

She was so pleased with her thriftiness

For this season she was to lovingly give

Thirty bright, shining, polished coins.

And they cast the same hue as the moonlight

Upon the drifts of fluffy, fallen snow.

About the Author

Born to a career United States Army officer and his wife, Rosalyn Rita Nicholas has lived at thirty-two addresses in her life. She lived in two foreign countries and nine states by the age of twenty-four. She graduated from Oklahoma State University in Stillwater, Oklahoma, with a bachelor's degree in English, meeting the grade point standard for Magna Cum Laude designation. Now retired, she worked many years in state government at a major social services agency writing statewide policy from federal regulations and state law. Rosalyn Rita Nicholas lives in Baton Rouge. She has been writing since youth.

Acknowledgment

I would like to thank my editor and publisher, James Clois Smith, Jr., of Sunstone Press for his belief in my work and the privilege to see my book come to life. I am deeply grateful for all of his efforts.